Original title:
Grapefruit Gaze

Copyright © 2025 Creative Arts Management OÜ
All rights reserved.

Author: Jaxon Kingsley
ISBN HARDBACK: 978-1-80586-461-5
ISBN PAPERBACK: 978-1-80586-933-7

Glistening Perspectives

In the morning light, a fruit does shine,
With a smile so bright, it's simply divine.
On the table it winks, a citrus delight,
Chasing worries away, oh what a sight!

Zesty peels tease, stories unfold,
With each silly bite, new tales are told.
Laughter erupts with the juice's splash,
Every squirt keeps the dull ashin' in trash.

The Sunrise's Embrace

Sunrise breaks, the kitchen's aglow,
A round citrus cheerleader, stealing the show.
Smiling so wide, on the breakfast plate.
This morning wonder won't make you late!

Squeezing it gently, a fountain appears,
A juice geyser bursts, filling hearts with cheers.
Every drop holds a giggle inside,
With each sip taken, joy cannot hide!

The Radiance of Peel

Orange and yellow, a sweater bright,
Wrapped so snug, in the morning light.
Peeling back layers, a slippery race,
Chasing its zest, such a lively space!

It rolls off the counter, a comical sight,
A citrus ball dancing, what pure delight!
Laughter erupts as it bumps to the floor,
Who knew breakfast could open such doors?

Juicy Inspirations

A fruity muse brings mischief to mind,
With each burst of flavor, new jokes intertwined.
Mixing sweet and sour, a wild refrain,
In the kitchen chaos, nothing's mundane.

Juicy inspirations, a blender's delight,
Swirling with giggles, what a funny sight!
Sip after sip, it's a laugh parade,
This funny fruit story will never fade!

Blushing Perspectives

A citrus blush upon my cheek,
It giggles soft, yet feels unique.
With every sip of morning sun,
I twirl and dance, I'm not yet done.

The fruit parade begins anew,
Each segment smiles, a playful view.
The tangy zest, a jester's grin,
In fruity worlds, I'll always win.

Tangy Daybreak

Morning light in citrus bursts,
Awakening my playful thirst.
A punchy twist in breakfast cheer,
I laugh aloud, 'It's time, my dear!'

The sunrise drips with fruity flair,
I splash and spill without a care.
Each slice a thrill, a wondrous tease,
This tangy daybreak brings me ease.

The Lush Look

Oh, luscious hue, what a delight,
Your vibrant shades are pure and bright.
With every slurp, I can't refrain,
The laughter bubbles up like rain.

A zesty wink, a cheeky slice,
You've got the charm, oh so precise.
In fruity fashion, I'm bemused,
With every glance, I'm so amused.

Awakening Aromas

Sweet scents arise to greet the day,
With whiffs of joy, they dance and sway.
A fruit parade in morning's light,
I chuckle at this fragrant sight.

Citrus laughter fills the air,
Enthralled by zest, I climb my stair.
Each drop of juice, a giggly cheer,
In this aroma, I find no fear.

Bitter-Sweet Insights

In the morning light, they seem quite odd,
Peeling back layers, a zesty facade.
Each slice reveals secrets, both tart and sweet,
A dance of confusion, a citrus treat.

Teetering joyfully on a balance beam,
Sour notes laugh back, a fruity theme.
With every bite, a giggle escapes,
As taste buds embrace their wild escapades.

A Citrus Lens

Through lenses of orange, I squint and see,
A world full of flavors, wild as can be.
Glimmers of laughter burst forth in zest,
Slicing through banter, we're truly blessed.

Jokes ripen daily in this twisty tree,
Where humor's a fruit, and smiles fly free.
Peeling away worries, I bask in the sun,
With each juicy moment, life's meant to be fun.

Radiant Meditations

Sitting cross-legged with a bowl of cheer,
Sipping on sunshine, dreams draw near.
Each segment a whisper of joy in the air,
Moments of laughter, nothing to compare.

Juicy reflections on the bright side of strife,
A citrus awakening, a fruity new life.
Giggles arise in this colorful brew,
With every bright smile, the world feels anew.

The Peel of Sunrise

As dawn breaks open, the peel rolls away,
Sunlight spills laughter, a brand new ballet.
Rays of bright humor tickle the skies,
While juiciness dances in fun little pies.

With each zesty morning, new mischief appears,
Spritzing of giggles, and playful cheers.
Beneath the bright peels, life's sweetly absurd,
In the garden of joy, we flourish undeterred.

Bright Orchard Whispers

In the orchard, laughter swells,
Juicy tales the fruit tree tells.
Peeling jokes in morning light,
Sunny pranks take off in flight.

With every bite, a giggle blooms,
Flavor dances, dispelling glooms.
Squirrels chuckle, a fruity jest,
Nature's comedy, at its best.

Sunkissed Reflections

Shadows play on citrus skin,
Brightly smiling, cheeky grin.
Sunshine spills like jelly jam,
Sticky sweet, oh what a slam!

The juice runs down our chins,
Tickling taste and cheeky grins.
A splash of zest in every scene,
Life is funny, pure and keen.

Zestful Glimpses

In the breeze, a tangy tease,
Bouncing laughs from tree to seas.
Squirrels dance with fruity flair,
Jokes as ripe as summer air.

Winking lemons lend a hand,
Dancing rhythms on the sand.
With each slice, hilarity
Unfolds in citrus clarity.

The Orange Horizon

Beyond the fields, a sunset spills,
Orange skies with playful thrills.
Whimsical clouds in fruity chase,
Tickling the sky with zesty grace.

As laughter rolls like waves of zest,
Nature's humor, truly blessed.
In the twilight, colors play,
A fun farewell to end the day.

Citrus Reverie

In the bowl a twist of fate,
A fruit so bright, oh, what a date!
With a smile and juicy grin,
I ponder where this day has been.

Pink and yellow, colors clash,
A citrus party, make a splash!
With every bite, a giggle bursts,
Why do we trust our taste buds first?

Slices of Sunrise

Morning rays bring zest anew,
Citrusy circles dance in view.
I slice and serve, a funny sight,
Why does my kitchen smell so bright?

My friend walks in, a puzzled face,
What's this odd and bright embrace?
We laugh, we taste, like kids at play,
Who knew breakfast could go this way?

The Bittersweet Stare

A citrus orb with glistening skin,
My eyes lock on, I can't begin.
A sip of juice, a scrunchy face,
Oh, the thrill of this wild chase!

"Too sour!" cries my friend in jest,
"Next time, let's avoid the zest!"
We share a laugh, then make a toast,
To fruits that tease us, we love most!

Pith and Petals

In a bowl of yellow cheer,
I spy a treasure, drawing near.
With petals bright and pith so bold,
A citrus tale in joy retold.

Ticks and tocks of fruity fun,
Who knew this could be number one?
A sunny slice that makes us grin,
And giggles bloom from deep within.

Citrus Mirage

In a world where zest runs free,
I tried to squeeze a sun-kissed tree.
But instead of juice, what did I find?
A cheeky squirrel, quite unrefined!

He grabbed my fruit with joyful flair,
Chased by birds that filled the air.
I laughed so hard, my cheeks turned red,
'That's not a breakfast!' I joyfully said.

Beneath the Peel

Peeling layers, oh what a chore,
Each strip revealing tales of yore.
A hidden note made me laugh out loud,
'Don't eat the seeds, they're not allowed!'

Beneath the skin, a silly song,
To dance and twirl, you can't go wrong.
The fruit of jest, in every bite,
Made breakfast feel delightfully light.

Sweet and Sour Memories

A childhood snack, oh so divine,
That tangy twist, a taste of shine.
I'd reach for slices, sticky and bright,
A citrus smile, a pure delight!

But one fateful morn, I bit in wrong,
The sweetness vanished, left me long.
A sour shock made me leap and twirl,
'This fruit's a prank!' I gave a whirl.

Morning's Zing

The sun peeked in with a citrus grin,
Awakening the day, let the fun begin!
I poured some juice in a bubbly cup,
And danced around, not wanting to stop.

The fizz and pop, a joyful cheer,
Went well with laughter, far and near.
Each sip a giggle, a playful tease,
Morning's zesty magic did as it pleased.

The Bold Slice

A citrus round with a vibrant hue,
I took a bite, and oh, how it flew!
Juice dripped down like a summer rain,
I laughed aloud, feeling no shame.

With each bold slice, my grin grew wide,
A funny dance, I couldn't hide.
The tartness tickled my funny bone,
In this fruity feast, I felt at home.

Golden Hour Reflections

In the golden light, it shone so bright,
A perfect orb, oh what a sight!
I peeled its skin and made a mess,
Laughter burst forth, I must confess.

Sweet and sour, a perfect blend,
These moments of joy, they never end.
Squirting juice like a water fight,
The orange blush under sunset light.

The Tantalizing Eye

Oh, what a tease, that citrus gleam,
It winks at me like a silly dream.
With each juicy bite, my belly laughs,
Who knew fruit could hold such halves?

The silly shapes, a gleeful spread,
A fruit for jest, a quirky bread.
I mix it up with a splash of flare,
This playful treat fills up the air.

Eyes of Citrus

Two eyes bright with a cheeky gleam,
A fruit's delight, a funny theme.
I poke and prod, it giggles back,
In this citrus world, there's never lack.

With zesty puns and fruity glee,
I squeeze out laughter, can't you see?
These eyes of citrus, sparky and bold,
In my silly heart, they take hold.

Visions in Coral

In the morning light, so bright,
A splash of pink, a citrus sight.
Faces twist in silly cheer,
As breakfast time draws us near.

With spoons in hand, we take a dive,
In a bowl where giggles thrive.
Rinds and pith, a tangy tease,
Who knew fruit could bring such ease?

The Juicy Horizon

Under the sun, we sip and slurp,
A storm of flavors with every burp.
Laughter dances in the air,
As zesty aromas swirl in flair.

Chasing wedges down the lane,
Sticky fingers, we feel no shame.
A citrus quest, our hearts ignite,
In this playful, fruity light.

Sunkissed Solitude

Alone I sit, but not for long,
A bright companion sings a song.
Its vibrant hues call out my name,
This citrus life is just a game.

Balancing on my spoon so tight,
A jiggly joy, a pure delight.
With each bite, my troubles wane,
I crack a smile, there's just no pain.

Citrus Whirl of Thoughts

A citrus whirl within my mind,
Sweet and sour, tangled entwined.
Fruits of laughter, peels of fun,
A zesty race just begun.

Every slice reveals a grin,
Juicy ponderings spin and spin.
Life's a party, let's not pout,
In this fruity world, we're blessed, no doubt!

Luminous Echoes

In a world where flavors grin,
The sun's a jester wearing skin.
Peeling laughter from the day,
Juicy secrets on display.

Splashes bright in morning light,
Bouncing giggles, taking flight.
Taste the tang upon your face,
Sour thoughts in a sweet embrace.

Citrus Horizons

A fruit parade with winking eyes,
Where zestful dreams twist and rise.
Laughing trees brew silly cheer,
As tangy thoughts draw us near.

In gardens ripe with citrus fun,
Everything is overrun.
With puns as fresh as morning dew,
Let the laughter bloom anew.

Eyeing the Sunrise

Morning yawns with citrus flair,
Waking up from fruity lair.
A wink of sun with sassy rays,
Chasing shadows of dull gray days.

With blushing tones that tease the sky,
Sour whispers float and fly.
As day unfolds, we giggle wide,
In bright hues, our joy can't hide.

Slices of Daydreams

Dreams are sliced in joyful chunks,
Jovial bursts and flavor hunk.
Citrus drips from lips so sly,
Where sticky giggles often lie.

Each segment tells a joke or two,
In zesty hues of every hue.
A fruit-filled laugh on every hand,
In silly moments, we take a stand.

Twilight in Citrus

In twilight's glow, the fruit does wink,
Orange and pink, what do you think?
It giggles softly, a zesty cheer,
Whispering secrets, oh so near.

Lemons tease with their sour frowns,
While limes plot, wearing their crowns.
A party in the orchard, what a sight,
Dancing citrus till the night.

Oranges roll down the grassy hill,
Chasing shadows, with zestful thrill.
They burst with laughter, peel in hand,
In this citrus world, they make their stand.

As stars begin to twinkle bright,
A fruit-filled frog jumps left and right.
Join this jest, come have some fun,
Twilight in citrus, the day's begun.

Coral Dawn Serenade

At dawn the coral fruit looks grand,
Winking at dreams, a merry band.
A melody floats through morning air,
Tangerine tunes beyond compare.

The sun arrives with a juicy grin,
Raising spirits, where to begin?
Fruit salads sing, in bowls they play,
Harmony found in every spray.

Lemon lights twinkle, a bright parade,
Citrusy jokes that never fade.
Banana splits dance on the lawn,
In this way, the day is drawn.

As colors swirl in bright display,
The coral dawn shouts hip-hip-hooray!
Join the fruit fiesta, don't delay,
A slice of joy is here to stay.

Fragrant Glimpses

In gardens where the fragrances mingle,
Citrus notes make the senses tingle.
A whiff of zest, a hint of glee,
These fruity pals are wild and free.

With peels like laughter, rolling round,
Oranges giggle without a sound.
Tart little berries join the fun,
Under the sunlight, everyone's spun.

Lemons swing in their citrus dance,
Inviting all to join the chance.
A fragrant glimpse, the laughter spreads,
Bringing joy to all who treads.

Bright juices drip with silly flair,
Creating smiles, in the warm air.
Let's toast with fruit, a zany feast,
Where every joke is just the beast!

The Vitamin Sea

In the vitamin sea, waves of zest,
Citrus surfers, they are the best.
Surfboards made of lime and orange,
Riding high, it's a funny forage.

Tangerines dive from peaks so steep,
Making splashes, in laughter, they leap.
With each citrus twist and juicy swirl,
The ocean shouts, "Let's dance and twirl!"

Coconut smiles with a nutty cheer,
Bananas sunbathe, shedding no fear.
All in this sea of fruity delight,
Silly antics under sunlight.

As the sun sets on this fruity spree,
The taste of laughter floats free like the sea.
Join the fun, let your spirits roam,
In the vitamin sea, you'll find a home.

A Citrus Conversation

Two halves share a sunny smile,
Juicy gossip in citrus style.
They giggle about their zesty life,
While dodging the knife of a morning strife.

Peels whisper secrets, sweet and bright,
Spilling tales of a fruitful night.
Their laughter echoes, tangy and bold,
In a bowl of sunshine, stories unfold.

Morning's Sweet Glare

The sun peeks in, a cheeky tease,
Waking up the sleepy trees.
A yellow orb in a fuzzy sky,
Pulls back the curtain with a little sigh.

Breakfast waits with a silly grin,
As citrus dreams begin to spin.
The morning light plays hide and seek,
While sweet scents dance, oh-so-unique.

Eyeing Sunlit Peels

In the corner, colors shine,
Pondering if this day is fine.
With a twirl and a twist, they sway along,
To a tangy tune, a cheerful song.

Their zest for life is quite the show,
With sunshine smiles, they steal the glow.
As nectar drops from laughs so pure,
The fruit bowl chuckles, that's for sure!

The Aroma of Awakening

Awake to scents that dance and sway,
A citrus serenade to start the day.
Bright beams peek in, a fruity bliss,
Each whiff a promise, a tasty kiss.

The kitchen hums with playful cheer,
A zesty chorus that draws you near.
With every slice, a wink delight,
Bringing giggles to morning light.

Sun-Kissed Shadows

In the garden bright and bold,
A fruit with secrets to unfold.
Peel it back, oh what a tease,
Sunshine smiles and citrus breeze.

A splash of zest, a wink of cheer,
Juice that dances, oh so near.
Sour and sweet, a playful fight,
Who knew fruit could bring such light?

Sticky fingers, laughter flows,
A citrus giggle, how it grows.
Under the sun, we take our stand,
With fruity fun that's truly grand.

The Flesh of Dawn

Morning breaks with a vibrant hue,
A burst of joy in every view.
Slice it slow, hear that squish,
A drippy joy is our first wish.

Bright and bold on the breakfast plate,
A zesty grin we just can't hate.
With each bite, the sun does rise,
In tangy laughter, our spirits fly.

A little squirt, an orange frown,
Eager tongues, ready to down.
Oh, the fun in every slice,
Makes our mornings oh so nice!

Radiance in Pink

Beneath the tree, a treasure waits,
Round and rosy, it celebrates.
A squishy globe, a sour delight,
Juicy giggles, morning's light.

In shades of pink, it loves to play,
Bouncing joy in a zesty way.
Fruitful quirks, oh what a scene,
Beauty wrapped in a juicy sheen.

Peel and munch, it's quite a game,
Fruits like this, they have no shame.
With every drop, a chuckle grows,
Radiant smiles, that's how it goes.

Eye of the Orchard

In the orchard, a watchful eye,
Round and plump, it catches the sky.
With every bite, it winks at me,
A zesty trick of nature's spree.

Sour bursts in a playful dance,
Within its skin, a daring chance.
With every slice, the laughter spreads,
Juicy tales, where fun embeds.

A citrus lens on a sunny day,
Bringing smiles in its own way.
So here's to the fun that we create,
With the eye that makes us celebrate!

The Citrus Sojourn

In the grove where fruits delight,
A citrus fellow, what a sight!
He juggles peels with joy so grand,
A zestful dance, a fruity band.

Lemon laughs as orange grins,
While limes spin tales of fruity sins.
A tango twist, a playful leap,
These citrus friends just love to keep!

The sun above, a golden smile,
Juicy joy stretches for a mile.
With every squeeze, a burst of cheer,
In this bright place, there's naught to fear.

And when the day taps out to rest,
The citrus crew feels truly blessed.
For every slice brings giggle fits,
A citrus sojourn full of wit.

Coral Hues of Morning

Morning breaks with coral glee,
A citrus crew, so wild and free.
They sip the sun, a cocktail blend,
With every sip, new jokes they send.

Orange bursts in laughter's rays,
And pinks declare a citrus craze.
Each bite of fruit sparks wacky tales,
As grapefruit sails on fruity jails.

Chasing roosters back to bed,
The citrus crew breaks out their spread.
With marmalade as parachute,
They laugh and roll, a joyful brute.

Coral shades paint skies above,
In this sweet world, we laugh and love.
Each juicy smile is a prize to boast,
In citrus hues, let's raise a toast!

The Nectar's Look

Nectar drips from happy trees,
A cheeky wink carried by the breeze.
Oh, look at that, the fruit's a tease,
Offering laughter with such ease.

Sticky fingers, giggles spread,
A jester's dance, our hearts are fed.
With every sip, a juicy quirk,
The nectar's look — oh, what a smirk!

Fruity friends in the morning light,
Making mischief, oh what a sight!
They trade sweet tales in between bites,
Creating joy in these fruity nights.

As day rolls on and laughter swells,
The nectar holds its fruity spells.
So grab a slice, come take a look,
In every drop, a brand new book!

Sunset Slices

As daylight dips, the sun turns gold,
Slices served, the fun unfolds.
Twilight giggles, a fruit parade,
With every laugh, good times displayed.

Peeling joy, the fruity friends,
Share citrus tales that never end.
A slice of lime, a pinch of zest,
In sunset hues, we feel our best.

As darkness falls, the stars ignite,
Fruit cups glow, oh what a sight!
With every slice, a sparkling cheer,
Sunset slices bring happiness near.

So gather round for fruity fun,
Under the glow, we're all as one.
With laughter shared, our hearts take flight,
In sugary bliss, we dance through night.

The Bold Eye

A citrus orb atop a stand,
It winks at me, oh isn't it grand?
With every slice, a secret shared,
Juicy laughs, I'm totally ensnared.

Its peels like jokes that twist and turn,
In zesty whims, my stomach churns.
I ponder life through vibrant skin,
What folly lies beneath the grin?

Citrus-Laced Thoughts

In a bowl of sunlight's hue,
Thoughts bubble up, a tangy brew.
What nonsense drips from citrus cheer?
A laugh so bright it's crystal clear.

Squeezed ideas spill and flow,
Like citrus juice, they brightly glow.
With every sip, a burst of fun,
These laced reflections weigh a ton!

Embracing the Zest

A zesty grin, a cheerful whiff,
I dance around, I'm full of spiff.
In juicy jests and leafy claps,
I twirl through life, no time for naps.

Each tangy bite, a giggle shared,
With zestful sprites, I'm gladly bared.
What folly brings this laugh parade?
In every squeeze, new jokes are made.

Citrus Cascade

A falling splash of sunny delight,
In citrus rain, I take my flight.
With every drop, a chuckle bright,
I leap and dance through zestful night.

As laughter pools in puddles wide,
In citrus waves, I surf the tide.
What wacky whimsy fills the air?
In fruity fun, I float without a care!

Juiced Perspectives

In the bowl, a citrus smile,
Peeling back a zesty style.
A splash of tart, sweet surprise,
Sipping sunshine through our eyes.

Wobbling like a jelly bean,
A fruit that's bold, yet so serene.
Dancing drips on kitchen tiles,
Giggling at its funky smiles.

Lemon's jealousy, oh so real,
Can't compete with this appeal.
A fruity joke, a clever pun,
It laughs and rolls, it's just such fun!

With every slice, quirky shapes,
Like a joker that escapes.
Life's a feast, so grab a spoon,
Let's toast to this fruity tune!

Vermilion Visions

Peeking through a ruby hue,
What nonsense does this fruit construe?
Juice runs wild, it spins and twirls,
Surely a prank in citrus swirls!

Lemon's worried, orange frowns,
While pink winks pull all the crowns.
Fruits unite in merry cheer,
Who knew this would bring such gear?

Sticky fingers, giggling fits,
A fruit that pulls off silly tricks.
A splash of juice, a burst of thrall,
It's the zaniest fruit of all!

With sloshing glee, we down the crush,
Fruity frolics make hearts rush.
Who knew a snack could cause such craze?
Life's absurd in vermilion rays!

A Fruitful Ponder

Sitting here, lost in thought,
This or that, what have I caught?
A tangy thought, a burst of zest,
What's life without a fruity quest?

Rinds of orange, tang of lime,
Tasting puddles won't waste time.
A splash of mischief on my cheek,
Fruit's giggle is what I seek!

My bowl of wonders full of glee,
It entertains just like a spree.
Squeeze a slice, let laughter flow,
In this ponder, chaos grows!

Squirty faces, juicy games,
Oh, what fun the citrus claims.
Take a bite, don't fear the mess,
Life's a laugh, just taste the zest!

Eyes Like Sunrise

Bright-eyed and bushy-tailed,
A bit of citrus never failed.
Morning laughs served on a plate,
All packed in a playful state.

Golden orb, a cheeky grin,
Who knew breakfast could begin?
Drinks of sunshine, broken rules,
Laughing lightly at our tools.

With every sip, a fruity cheer,
A wink to sunlight ever near.
Day has dawned with zest and bite,
A whimsical way to greet the light!

So let's embrace this peppy laugh,
In our hearts, let joy take half.
Squirt a bit, giggle away,
Eyes like sunrise lead the way!

The Essence of Zest

In the morning light, a twist of fate,
A citrus sun on my breakfast plate.
Bright and bold, a burst of fun,
Dancing juice in the kitchen run.

Under the peel, a wink and grin,
With every slice, the laughter spins.
It's a tangy joke in the midday haze,
Squeezing smiles in zesty waves.

Rolling thoughts like a fruit on a spree,
Zingy moments, wild and free.
Sunshine fizzing in a glass, oh dear,
Tip it back and shed a tear.

So grab a wedge and take your stand,
Join the giggles, citrus and hand.
Life's a punch, a tangy jest,
In the essence of zest, we are blessed.

Citrus Sorcery

A wizard's hat of orange hue,
Stirring potions from morning dew.
With a flick of wrist, a splashy scene,
It's fruit enchantment, and oh so keen.

Lemon drops and limey tricks,
Dancing shadows with zestful kicks.
Every sip, a bubbling laugh,
Slipping flavors in a silly craft.

Peels like capes upon the floor,
Citrus capers we can't ignore.
A jester's grin in the fragrant air,
Life's a jibe when you dare to share.

So raise your glass, let's toast tonight,
With flavors swirled, what a delight!
In this juicy magic, hearts entwine,
Citrus sorcery is simply divine.

In the Wake of Flavor

Waking up to citrus delight,
A juicy jolt to start the flight.
With every bubble, giggles rise,
Teasing taste buds with pleasant surprise.

A splash of color on the tongue,
Songs of sweetness, lightly sung.
In the wake of flavors so bold,
Stories unfold as the zest takes hold.

Softly dripping, a sunny cheer,
Banishing shadows, brightening fear.
Life's a journey on this citrus wave,
Splashing humor, oh how we crave!

Peel back laughter, let it shine,
Squeeze out the fun, every drop divine.
In the wake of laughter, hearts will play,
Joy bubbles forth, come what may.

A Palette of Pulp

Colors swirling in vibrant hues,
Crafting zany, juicy news.
With every bite, a quirky tale,
Pulp-filled stories that never fail.

Chasing bits of tangy zest,
Every fruit knows what's best.
A squeeze of humor here and there,
We're painting life without a care.

With every wedge, a giggle shared,
In the citrus chaos, we're all prepared.
A splash of laughter, and off we go,
In a world where the bright fruits glow.

So let's create with zest and flair,
A palette of pulp, if you dare.
For in this mixing bowl of love,
The joys of life are sent from above.

The Fruitful Stare

With citrus depths, a glance so bright,
It catches eyes, like sun at night.
Peeling back layers, what will you find?
A zesty laugh that's sweetly blind.

In a world of lemons, I'll take my shot,
A playful wink, I've got the lot.
And in this moment, laughter flows,
For fruity fun, that's how it goes.

Sipping juice beneath the trees,
Giggling softly in the breeze.
A juicy jest, a sweetened tease,
In citrus bliss, we find our ease.

So join the fun, don't look away,
In every bite, a laugh to play.
With vibrant hues that make us sing,
A fruitful stare, oh what joy it brings!

Sunlit Eyewear

I wear my shades on a sunny day,
To block the rays and make them play.
Each lens a portal to brighter sights,
Where every joke takes flight and bites.

Covered eyes and laughter loud,
With citrus tones, I feel so proud.
As colors swirl, and giggles fly,
My sunny specs reflect the sky.

A fleeting glance, a wink to share,
The world awash in fruity flair.
So bring your best and make it bright,
With sunlit fun, we'll dance all night.

A playful twist, a citrus spin,
With every laugh, we dive right in.
These lenses hold a world of cheer,
In every sunny face, we find our gear!

Tangerine Glare

A tangerine swirl, with zest to spare,
Catches attention with a comical glare.
Round and bright, like a clownish face,
In this fruit basket, we find our place.

Lively laughs in a citrus pose,
Do you feel that? A jester's toes!
With every chuckle, the world feels right,
As puns and smiles take to flight.

Tangerine tricks, oh what a treat,
In fruity fun, we feel the beat.
So join the dance, let the laughter soar,
With every glance, we'll ask for more.

The glow of orange lights the way,
Through jolly moments, come what may.
With giggles shared, we break the mold,
In tangerine glare, stories unfold!

Coral Visions

Coral shades paint the world today,
With fruity hues that lead the play.
In visions bright, the laughter swells,
As we spin tales that charm and tell.

With every sip, a twist awaits,
A fruity journey through vibrant gates.
Lemon drop giggles and berry skies,
In coral dreams, hilarity flies.

A whirlwind of colors, a zesty spree,
Invite your friends; just you and me.
Let's revel in joy, as we laugh and cheer,
With visions sweet, there's nothing to fear.

So take a look at the world ahead,
With coral shades, no tears are shed.
In every smile, a sunny ray,
In fruity mirth, we find our way!

Echoes of Tartness

In a world where flavors clash,
Tartness wears a sneaky mustache.
Puckered lips and laughter bright,
Who knew sour could feel so right?

A juggling act of citrus zest,
Fruits in hats, they do their best.
Gladly slipping, tripping too,
Tart is just a party hue!

Spritz of zest, a fruit parade,
Sour notes in sunlight played.
Fruity giggles fill the air,
Life's a joke, but who would care?

With each bite, we grow more bold,
Sour secrets waiting to be told.
Echoes of laughter, tart and clear,
In every slice, we find the cheer!

The Color of Joy

Gleeful hues that catch the eye,
Bouncing slices zooming by.
Juicy bursts of yellow round,
With every peel, new laughs are found.

A splash of color, bright delight,
It dances in the morning light.
Witty puns and zesty jokes,
Citrus dreams and sunny folks!

With every sip of sunlit cheer,
We toast to laughter, no more fear.
A fruity frolic, sweet and spry,
Raise a glass, let spirits fly!

Wonders hidden in each hue,
A tangy twist, an orange view.
Colorful smiles, in every bite,
The taste of joy that feels so right!

Twilight's Citrus Touch

As dusk descends with citrus flair,
Lemon lights up with a cheeky stare.
In twilight's glow, the laughter swells,
A fruity riddle, no one tells.

Jokes on the tongue, flavors collide,
Sour dreams we cannot hide.
Twisted laughter in every peel,
Citrus humor makes us squeal!

Under starry skies, we grin,
Tartness dances, let the fun begin.
With every slice, we spin and twirl,
In twilight's grip, it's a citrus world!

So raise your fruit, don't miss the chance,
In this tangy, zesty dance.
Twilight's touch, a sweet embrace,
Laughter ripples in every space!

Sunlit Segments

Sunlit segments, bright and round,
Slice of happiness, magic found.
Tart explosions in the air,
With every bite, jokes everywhere!

Witty wedges pave the way,
For giggles shared throughout the day.
A juicy grin, a happy cheer,
In citrus quirks, we persevere!

Golden rays, the fruit parade,
Sour smiles that never fade.
A punchline hidden in each taste,
Make haste, don't let this go to waste!

Sunlit laughter on our plates,
Tartness jests as joy awaits.
In every segment, a playful tease,
Life's a laugh, just sip with ease!

The Art of Observance

In a bowl there sits a treat,
With a pucker that can't be beat.
I squint to see its zesty grin,
Wondering just where to begin.

Tartness dances on my tongue,
With laughter, I feel so young.
Juice squirts like a playful jest,
This citrus fruit is truly blessed.

People gather, eyes aglow,
Each slice a story to bestow.
I watch them munch, a bright parade,
Planning schemes that we have laid.

Neighbors pop in for a taste,
Not one morsel goes to waste.
As I observe their cheeky bites,
I share in giggles, pure delights.

Savory Sunsets

The sun dips low, a juicy hue,
Splashes of pink and yellow too.
With every bite, the colors swirl,
Nature's circus in a twirl.

Sipping nectar, laughs erupt,
My friends and I, delight erupt.
Peeling layers, what a sight,
Citrus smiles in soft twilight.

A toast to zing, we share a slice,
The sunset's tang, a sweet surprise.
We giggle as the seeds take flight,
Dancing dreams in golden light.

Packing up, but spirits soar,
With laughter ringing, we want more.
In dusk's embrace, our hearts collide,
Savoring moments, side by side.

Slices of Serenity

On a plate, a sunburst waits,
Offering peace, tempting fates.
Its skin, a canvas, bright and bold,
A tale of zest, yet to be told.

As I slice, the juice cascading,
A citrus waterfall invading.
Each segment whispers soft delight,
In every angle, pure insight.

Friends gather 'round, it's quite a scene,
Unwrapping giggles, feeling keen.
With every joke, the flesh revealed,
In laughter's grip, our hearts are healed.

So here's to joy, in fruity bites,
And silly moments, sheer delights.
A simple fruit, yet oh so grand,
We savor life, hand in hand.

The Celestial Citrus

A starry fruit from cosmic lands,
With bursts of brightness in my hands.
Planets spin with every bite,
In fruity realms, we take flight.

I laugh at all the sour faces,
As tangy juice creates wild races.
Friends burst in with playful cheers,
A tournament of silly jeers.

The table's set; it's quite the view,
With cosmic slices, tried and true.
Each glowing orb, a tasty ride,
Chasing flavors, side by side.

So let's toast to our zesty fling,
In humors charm, our souls take wing.
With every nibble, memories bloom,
In the citrus glow, we find our room.

Radiance in Bloom

In morning sun, I squeeze and grin,
A fruity sport, let the laughter in.
With pithy jokes and zesty cheer,
This citrus day, oh so dear!

Beneath the skin, a treasure bold,
Tangy tales waiting to be told.
I toss the seeds, they fly like stars,
In my backyard, forget the cars!

My taste buds dance, a wild parade,
Each slice a smile, laughter displayed.
A tart reminder, life's a game,
With every bite, I stake my claim.

So grab a knife and take a chance,
Let citrus joy lead this sweet dance.
In radiant bloom, we'll laugh and play,
With every sip, brighten the day!

The Ornate Peel

A twisted peel, a crown so bright,
Like funny hats in morning light.
I wear it proud, my citrus crown,
Dancing as I stroll through town.

Each segment smiles, my tastebud friend,
With zestful tales that never end.
People gawk, my fruit parade,
While I munch with a citrus charade!

Juicy splatters, giggles too,
As citrus kingdoms come in view.
No dullness here, oh what a thrill,
I'll toss the peel, give laughter a spill!

So take a sip of sunshine bright,
Let's toast to joy, with all our might.
In ornate peels, we find our muse,
In fruity bliss, we cannot lose!

Citrus Echoes in Silence

In quiet corners, citrus sings,
With whispers sweet of zesty things.
A silent laugh, a juicy punch,
When life is dull, I'll take a crunch.

Colors bright, a citrus hymn,
A playful note that piques the whim.
Each bite a joke, a comic blend,
In fruity moments, laughter's friend.

Oh, tangy scents float in the air,
As giggles dance without a care.
Bright citrus smiles, a cheeky tease,
In echoes soft, we find our ease.

So as the silence sings along,
I'll hum a tune, a fruit-filled song.
In citrus echoes, we'll delight,
With every bite, life feels just right!

The Whisper of Citrus

A whisper soft, a citrus cheer,
Tales of tanginess draw me near.
When life gets sour, I'll burst with zest,
In citrus realms, I find my rest.

Juicy tales, a twist of fate,
With every nibble, I celebrate!
In secret gardens, fruits abound,
The whispering joy is all around.

Lemon laughs and orange schemes,
In dreamy days, the fruit world gleams.
With every slice, hilarity flows,
In playful bliss, my spirit glows.

So let's embrace this citrus spree,
With giggles shared, just you and me.
In the whisper of fruit, we'll soar,
With laughter ripe, forevermore!

Fading Citrus Light

In a kitchen bright, fruits take flight,
Lemons take aim, a zesty delight.
Orange peels slip, their secrets entwine,
While limes laugh loud, with a twist of the rind.

Tangerine tango, a dance on the shelf,
They grin at the fridge, their juiciness stealth.
The lemons all whisper, 'We're scarily sweet!'
As zest fills the air, oh, what a treat!

A citrus parade, rolling down the lane,
With grapefruits winking through the windowpanes.
Bananas are jealous, all yellow and shy,
As oranges chuckle, "Come join us! Oh my!"

So laugh with your fruit, let the laughter flow,
In this citrus world, where silliness grows.
With every bright slice, a chuckle we'll find,
In this fading light, oh, citrus combined!

The Glow of Citrus Dreams

Under the glow of a citrus dream,
Limes roll around, giggling, it seems.
Oranges joke, 'We're the best in the pack!'
But lemons retort, 'We've got tang on our back!'

In a bowl of delight, they all gather near,
Whispering secrets for the hungry to hear.
With citrusy antics, they play hide and seek,
Hiding behind apples, those fruity little freaks!

Citrus clowns jive with the figs and the pear,
Swapping their stories without any care.
A grapefruit nods, 'I'm the life of this bash!'
While cherries look on, 'Oh, they're really quite rash!'

So let's squeeze the joy from these zesty friends,
With laughter and smiles that never quite ends.
In a glow of fruit dreams, we dance and we twirl,
Amidst citrus delights, we'll give life a whirl!

Citrus Dreams

In a citrus dream where the laughter's loud,
Peeling the layers, oh, I feel so proud!
With oranges giggling, limes twist and prance,
Grapes roll their eyes at this fruity romance.

Under the sun, they flaunt their bright hues,
Mangoes whisper secrets that nobody knew.
Citrus adventures down lemony lanes,
Where laughter is juicy, and joy never wanes!

Tossing the slices like confetti of fun,
These citrusy pranks, oh, they've hardly begun!
In gardens of zest, we'll dance in a line,
With berries behind us, all feeling divine!

So cherish these moments, as sweet as a dream,
In this fruity world, nothing's quite as it seems.
With giggles and grins, we'll savor the spree,
In citrusy realms, wild and fancy-free!

Juicy Reverie

In a reverie bright, of colors so bold,
Citrus fruits chatter, their stories unfold.
With laughter and zest, they share their sweet cheer,
As grapefruits chuckle, "Come join us right here!"

They bounce on the counter, a lively parade,
Oranges flip flopped, not a moment delayed.
Lemons burst out, "We're the sours to aid!"
While apples just sigh, feeling slightly outplayed.

In juicy delight, they sprinkle their grace,
With limes that do cartwheels, a dance full of base.
The tangy brigade, they savor the day,
With fruity shenanigans, come join the fray!

So let's savor life, with a wink and a twist,
In this juicy reverie, something you can't miss.
With laughter and flavor, oh what a grand show,
In a world of vivid fruit, let the good times flow!

Fruitful Contemplation

In the kitchen, I ponder, so bright,
Round and bouncy, a citrus delight.
Should I squeeze it for juice, or just eat?
It might wear my shirt, oh, isn't that neat?

Slicing in half, it offers a grin,
Juicy and tart, like a cheeky twin.
It rolls off the counter, a bold little dare,
Is this fruit laughing, or just unaware?

Zest fills the air, my taste buds awake,
It's a fruit party here, make no mistake.
With each little bite, I munch with glee,
Citrus whimsy is the life for me!

A twist of the knife, a splash of bright zest,
Even lemons envy this citrus best!
Funny how fruit can bring such cheer,
Next time, I'll invite all my pals here!

Daring Citrus Stares

Sitting in sun with confidence bold,
A fruit in my hand, just waiting to unfold.
It blinks at me, a dare so sly,
'Do you think you can handle my bright, zesty high?'

Peeling my snack, a tango I dance,
The juice springs forth, oh, what a chance!
I giggle and snicker at its citrus charm,
Thankful my clothes have escaped from harm.

With a challenging wink, it rolls on the floor,
Should I catch it, or just let it explore?
It bounces with laughter, a true little sprite,
Who knew that breakfast could be such delight!

I ponder its essence, all tart and sweet,
In this citrus showdown, who'll take the seat?
Witty and juicy, I'm in on the fun,
This daring fruit might just be number one!

Evoking the Essence

Bright yellow skin, a smile so wide,
With every fresh slice, it's hard to hide.
It winks at the sunlight, oh what a tease,
Can I handle the zing that's meant to please?

A skit in the kitchen, my fruit takes a stand,
With a squeeze and a squirt, it's hilariously planned.
The essence of fun, it splashes around,
Juicy adventures in laughter abound.

"Hey, taste me!" it shouts, "I promise, it's bliss!"
But oh, the pucker, it's hard to dismiss!
Yet giggles ensue, what a comical plight,
Citrusy chaos when I take a bite!

It's the laughter of mornings, the joy on my plate,
A friendship with fruit, I can hardly await.
Mixing and mingling, zest spices the day,
Evoking my thoughts in the silliest way!

The Essence of Dawn

Morning sun spills through my kitchen door,
With vibrant orbs perched on the floor.
A citrusy dance in a glass by my side,
What mischief awaits with this morning tide?

Bright colors cheer, as I slice and I dice,
Each tangy little piece, a swing of nice spice.
They giggle and shimmer, with laughter they sing,
"Join us, dear friend, for a bright citrus fling!"

Juice splashes and squirts, like a playful prank,
I try to remain calm, but I chortle and tank!
What fun to assemble this fruity delight,
As I sit with my breakfast, it feels so right.

The dawn is a canvas, with colors to whirl,
Each slice is a heartbeat, a playful swirl.
Sipping the essence, a sunrise in cheer,
Laughing with fruit, as the day draws near!

A Taste of Dawn

Morning breaks with citrus cheer,
A splash of zest, I tip my beer.
My breakfast fruit wears a bright grin,
Check out that peel - where to begin?

Sunshine calls from kitchen bright,
Orange hopes in the morning light.
Slice it up, a twist of fate,
Syrupy sweet, don't make me wait!

Jovial bites bring smiles so bold,
Wonders of fruit in colors untold.
With every squeeze, a splash of fun,
Who knew dawn could taste like a pun?

So raise your glass, let's have a toast,
To zesty dreams we love the most.
With laughter ripe, the day unfolds,
Citrus laughter never gets old.

Through Fruity Lenses

Beneath the sun and fruity dreams,
I squint a bit, or so it seems.
Lens of laughter, life's bright frame,
Oranges glowing, it's all a game.

A twist and turn, a fruit parade,
Lemons frown – oh, what a charade!
Slice through the haze of morning brew,
Sipping sunshine, giggles ensue.

Visions blurred in juicy frames,
All my friends are fetching names.
With every sip, reality bends,
Is it juice or jest? It all depends.

Through fruity lenses, colors collide,
Citrus sparkles, no place to hide.
Life's a punchline of joy and zest,
In this crazy world, we're truly blessed.

The Orchard's Secret

Whispers run from tree to tree,
An orchard secret calls to me.
Juicy rumors ripe with glee,
What's the scoop? Let's climb and see!

Fruits conspire in shades of blush,
Giggling leaves in a midday hush.
Each branch holds a tale, a jest,
Funky flavors, do your best!

Peeling back the layers of fun,
Sour sparkles, that's how it's done.
From nectar sweet to tangy bite,
Every flavor stirs delight.

Behind the trunk, hidden treasures,
Laughter's found in nature's measures.
Folks will wonder, what's the key?
A fruity riddle, come taste with me!

Juxtaposition of Juices

In a world where flavors clash,
Minty greens meet a tangy splash.
Pineapple licks the tartest lime,
Mix it right, we're having a rhyme!

Juices fight in a frothy race,
Pomegranate smiles, holds a strong face.
Coconut joins, all laid back,
Sipping on dreams, there's no lack.

A swirl of chaos, taste sensation,
Life's combining in this creation.
From zest to sweet, a merry blend,
With every sip, the giggles extend.

Juxtaposed in colors so bright,
A battle of fruits, pure delight.
So let's pour out this fruity spree,
Laughter flows with every sunny spree!

www.ingramcontent.com/pod-product-compliance
Lightning Source LLC
Chambersburg PA
CBHW060125230426
43661CB00003B/339